I0836412

FOR NOAH

Trillion Amber Trumpets
Arkansas Queer Poet Series #3

Cover photograph: found photograph, photographer unknown

Cover design by Seth Pennington

Sibling Rivalry Press, LLC
159 Sunset Drive
North Little Rock, AR 72118

info@siblingrivalrypress.com

www.siblingrivalrypress.com

ISBN: 978-1-943977-93-2

First Sibling Rivalry Press Edition, April 2026

Trillion Amber Trumpets

JC Andrews

SIBLING RIVALRY PRESS
DISTURB/ENRAPTURE
LITTLE ROCK, ARKANSAS

POEMS

NETTIE

The okra, right now, all heart,
is putting on its flowers
underneath her voice, which,
I swear, makes the trees
stop growing for however
many seconds she decides
to talk about how the phone
lines used to be connected,
and more particularly,
about how she would
eavesdrop on Jeanette's
conversations, although
when Jeanette died,
she had her phone line
disconnected, because
the only person she talked
to on the landline anymore
was Jeanette, who called
her every single day
and lived two minutes
down the road, across
from the window I used
to crawl out of to meet
girls who I thought
had angels stirring
inside them, for which
I was probably right,
and for which I was sorry,
but I was under the type
of sky that doesn't care
what you're sorry for,
which is the type of sky
I'm under now, which is
a sky that rolls me and rolls
me, saying look at how pure
I am without trying, and how
I love nothing, and how
I can never get caught.

TRINKET I

humans are cause
animals we are always
hunting for a cause
maybe it's
the rain
coming in
like an empty
chapel or just
the clean algebra
of the sky that
reminds me
I am not
completely
uninterested in
the notion of flight
but my inability
to grow a set
of wings: mercy

FLORISSANT

No, not again. Not the shimmering
funk of the evening seeping between
the radiant gears of the sky that couple
and click into days, that click into months,
that click into the kind of loneliness
you feel you must have known
but forgotten about. Not the army
of daffodils forming a soft membrane
around the luckier half of the cemetery.
Not the awkward windup of spring
or its many fuchsia knuckles.
Not the windchime making opera
of its body in the april tomb. Not the rain,
again. Not the clouds rolling light like
candelabras. Not the electric bell
of a tangerine. Not the drawl of starlings
ringing out in all directions. Not the way
you think of one silo until you see
the next. Not the music and cake again.
Not the oven of my body churning out
its useless hours. Not the tickseed laced field
building its plain language in my heart. No,
not my stupid heart, not how it slackens
itself against the bangery of years.

REMEMBERING OURSELVES OVER

you can take your trotline
all the way to god and let
this tomboy who's run it
already pray that she can
soul around her body
in the tub so her own
freaky beat of youth
can turn luscious what
if you put rock salt in her
bottom lip like sinners make
her remember how she spit it
like her daddy now pretending
she was the man with tobacco
for the bee stings stretching
her architecture out toward
the stars in her heart there
is a language we all
miss in the distance
of that language
is longer than
the work hour
you are older than
you think you are
and stinking of your
name imagine your name
in your own body your body
does not imagine your name what
is your name if not an instrument for
becoming less attached to your hands

TRINKET II

electricity has something
to do with your life
the shock of hearing
your name is
the same
place you
come from
you are allowed to
believe in everything
you can look back
and know again
look forward
and think
I will grind
blooms from
whatever I lack
the same way
my face turns
toward the light
by instinct

MISS YOU CONTRAPUNTAL

do I still	remind you	of your father
hold on	or else I will	tell the truth
to your	face	which is
beautiful	enough to be	machinery
glistening	in rewind	like the brains of
angels	forever	the sweetest
of questions	like are you real	god
like are you	enough to be	working out
sad	(ness)tled in	the coordinates of heaven
as the sound of	stars	silently and worn down
hums	and barbed wire	sits tender like please
touch me	babydoll	give me
somewhere	I can lay	my head
down	hay along	back
roads where	my hands	remember
the stupid	sleep	of my heart
cattle lie down	before it rains	I am
lonely but	it seems I am	in charge
of this life	given out	at random and
must rest	remind me	to tell you
what hurts	about loving	is long

TRINKET III

horses only lie down
for REM sleep they nap
standing up to protect
themselves only open
enough to say they
are unfinished
somewhere
maybe there is
someone waiting
for you like that I read
in Augustine's Confessions
that the senses are the body's
gates the concept of a gate
originally referred to a gap
in the wall or fence rather
than the barrier that
closed it what
then is an
open mouth
I think most
of us we want
to be good to
each other

EVEN WITH

"Mercy is a verb. / Mercy, mercy, call off th dogs / it's just me, remember—"
- Cody-Rose Clevidence, "Cygnus th Swan"

I crawl under the door
to the smokehouse
where, for whatever
reason, the hunting
dogs like to hide,
and I sit in the dirt
with their heads
in my lap while
I pinch together
the skin between
their shoulder blades
and stick in the needle.
From outside, I hear
my grandfather tell
one of my uncles
I'm the only
one they'll let
close enough
to touch.

I lean back against
the wall and look
at the other wall
feeling good
about hearing
him say it.
The dogs curl
up in the corner,
and I dig my heels
in the ground.
It's damp in here,
and the poles hung
from the ceiling
are stained from
last year's sausage.
I'm old enough now
to be wearing a bra.

When I pull myself
back out again, I feel
my chest scrape
against the bottom
of the door. The sun
makes a silhouette
of my uncle's hand
reaching down
toward me,
and I grab it.
His smile makes
me nervous,
but he can play
the harmonica,
which somehow
makes me less.
In the house,
my grandmother
picks the bones
from a can of salmon.
She likes to make
fun of my teeth.

In the mirror,
I pull up my top
lip, and it makes
me mad. I remember
the first time
I touched myself
in this bathroom,
and it makes me
want to do it
again, and while
I do, I hear
my cousin
in the back
calling every
car that passes
in his video
game a queer.

I can't put a name
to how sick I am
of my own two
hands already.
There's a pear
tree outside
I haven't quite
figured out
how to climb.
Today, the number
on the ground
is forty-two.
The number
of pears.

When I pick
one up to throw
at the fence,
I get so angry
that I don't,
and then I just
get sad, but before
I can get angry
enough again
to actually
throw it,
one of the dogs
walking toward
me looking like
if I touched
her she'd break
into a fury
of blooms.

TRINKET IV

my aunt T
holds my face
and really looks
at it before she
kisses me it's like
a language under
the one I know
how light
is in small
houses is
of that same
grammar the way
grass grows on graves
is of it too first there's
nothing and then
there is a life
laid over
a life

YOU SAY WHAT'S WRONG I SAY AN EYELASH

October, you feel ancient. I wake up in you and look in the mirror where, unwillingly, I must confront my nervous history, which is more meaningful, say, than my more delicate anxieties, such as running into my neighbor on the way out the door or saying something stupid on the phone later. I do give a terrific shit I've realized, and although unadorned, I am heavy with the battlefield of my more curious thoughts. I run my fingers along a comb, you see, and think of a filet knife along a fish's ribs, which is recklessly specific, don't you think, given that I know myself to be as sensitive as a piano and to the touch respond similarly. My dumb blood, my stubborn inklings, my head whistling on forever. Just now, I remember firefly innards glowing on the palms of my hands, and therefore must recall how they look floating through the cemetery. I think the dead are of an ilk as vibrant as that, and they live on cold melon, and they have no memories. I think a grave with no name yet is how I feel about music, or better yet, I think music is spontaneous architecture not unakin to the thick systems of my heart which maps pulsations across my body as it moves among pills, lavender, concrete.

TRINKET V

a hive of stars
a dark field a low
moon hanging onto it
like a white petal swarms
of indigo dragonflies
cobwebs you can
only see when
the dew has set
just enough to take
the edge off of everything
that night in your sleep
a dream where your mother
sits at the foot of your bed
and plays a mute
instrument
you can't put
a name to

LIKE A LAMP SOMEBODY LEFT ON

if children's
voices were
not so goddamn
moving if they
were not so
crackly

like stars if I
could reach
the chest in
my chest if
my mother
was interested
in albatrosses or
just the barn
owl behind her
eyes if I grew up
where trains ran
if I looked back
and got full inside
if the water did
not half baffle
me every time
I saw it if
the moose
in my dreams
would stop
banging its head
against my window
if these little touches
of solitude in me
if I could
arrange them
in such a way
that they were
countable or
just seeable even
if the blank
white zinnias
did not make me
so sad if my body
could find
its zero
degree

if I could
knock over
the moon if
technology did
not sometimes
really touch me
if my grandmother's
text messages did
not make me
believe in god
if the rain
would stop
lifting
the quieter
drums from
the earth if
the microscopic
excellences
of the sound
of lying down
in between
two rows
of corn did not
remember me
the same way
in which
I remember
it which is
young
breathing
and deeply
invisible

if the porch light
did not make such
a gown around
me if I did
not want so
badly to
make things
beautiful
for you
mother
if I could
say something

that really matched
the look in your
eyes if the buffalo
fish could tell us
how it lives
so long if
Big John's
pinky ring
wasn't stuck
in the ground
with him
if death was
undoable thus
less radiant
therefore
easier to
swallow
I like
you want
to know what
I'm willing
to admit

if I wasn't
so interested
in how words
bust holes
through us
the same way
a grapevine
rises up
to pierce
its place
in the earth
I would have
stopped trying
if I didn't
remember
looking up
at the church
fans before
I could talk
if I didn't
imagine
peacefulness
like snow

underwater
if there was
a way to
make it
real if I
could get past
the idea of making
it real if I could
be satisfied with
how close I get
when hearing
a piano if
I wasn't such
a chickenshit
the day Sophia
asked me

to flip over
the boat
by the pond
if I was
less afraid
of what's
under
things

TRINKET VI

my grandmother is
a hoarder in a small
home so when she makes
pasta she has nowhere
to put it other
than the beds
sometimes
I would
come in
from school
to find it drying
under the ceiling
fan in her room
does a quiet like
that leave some
thing in your
heart

UNORGANIZE THIS MOTHERSHIP

unangel this house
I'm sick of this house
being angeled
with kitchen
ghosts

You almost got
zenithified by
me except I
realized we
are just
little
spaces
taking
up
space
you should
know how
to buffalo
fish by now

B
ut
you
are still
afraid
of wat
er because
it is
so re
arranging
you rearrange me
though so
give me a break
I wish you didn't
feel so cathedral
or like a loose form
ula or like a feeling
in my gut but here I am
dreaming one of those dreams
you feel awake for and you are
spread out on nonna's table
and I am looking over your shoulder
and nonna is dead but I see her
all hunkered down
and looking at me
from the doorway
of the closet in the kitchen
and suddenly you grab your chest
and say my name in a voice
that makes my body
stop to move

oh
holy
water
and
rain
bows
in
so
many
cor
ners

can we stop feeling a
round these lanky
stars of our bodies
and finding our
mothers or
what

The
first
mem
ory
I have
of
you
is
hid
ing
in the
closet
while
you
holl
er
my
name
like
it is
some
thing
you
want
to
un
be
lieve

TRINKET VII

a fig is not a fruit
but an inflorescence
pollinated by a mother
wasp laying her thousand
little eggs inside they all
die and turn to seed
except for the daughters
who crawl out looking
for somewhere else to put
down their lives each night
my mother leans
against the counter
like a photo
of someone I love
a keepsake that makes
it easier somehow
to love them

I DO NOT UNDERSTAND MY INSTRUMENT

for AB

The way the hills repeat themselves is my angel. I can't
duck it. The purr of grass grates against distant engines.

The dogs run. Their hard breath multiplies the garnet light.
The garnet light lowers itself into the stuttering wheat field.

The stutter deepens. What if I die. I want them to say
You were terrible. We loved you. Oh, and this is enough,

just for the record, the garnet light and the stutter,
for me. My grandmother has not traveled very far.

She found her father dead in the cucumbers. There is
a boneless blue dark she is waiting for. I return here

so my heart can sharpen itself on the low rub of her
voice. No more mirrors. I'm listening to the corn.

Tell me we don't have to look at each other, please.
If I ask you to put me out to pasture, what then.

TRINKET VIII

the loneliness you feel
in the garden makes you
suddenly responsible for
the rest of your life
and how it
changes you
is not magnificent
it's more like
a wish you make
to nail someone's shoes
to the floor except
they are your shoes
except they are
your father's
except they are
on your feet when
you look down
and you can't
stop yourself
from laughing
but when you laugh
everything else
is so quiet
you feel
the need
to stop

OZARKS

we all have boy cousins we are afraid of we all sit in class
and want to fuck we took the bus we took a photo sitting
on the bed we stole each other's hearts again uh oh
our fathers are drunk and we are in the wheat field
playing who wants to touch me tomorrow
we will run four miles and go to church
afterwards our grandmothers will fry things
we are shy and muscled up we live in homes
that smell like water we eat red meat
and sound like the women we love
we touch palms to measure up our coach
is creepy we watch lightning roll across
the foothills and hear the dogs bark
we know the radio in the garden
doesn't work we cut ourselves
like the girls on TV do we buy
beer from our older brothers we
sit on the fence and drink up
we talk in the dark we
talk in the dark we talk
we want to start a fire
in the driest part
of August we see
ourselves in the first
headlights of the night
look how close we
are now stop

TRINKET IX

laughing we would count
out nine chickens
in the dark me
and this girl
from Clinton
I can't remember
her name but she was
beautiful and working
most nights at Sonic
except for chicken
catching nights
ten dollars
an hour cash plus
twenty every hour
we stayed past eleven
afterwards I'd go home
and check my mother's vitals
before I got drunk in the shed
I was tired and loved the way
my face felt new under
my fingers when I thought
about the girl
touching it

HOPE CARVES

I think about the curve on highway nine all the time
where, if you
can catch it, the sunlight hits the sage grass so right,
the earth feels
more real, like when it's raining, but there, I mean
in the curve,
it doesn't have to be raining for the earth to feel more
real, because
there is the toothless light and the field waving
its trillion
amber trumpets, because the field is not fearful
of cattle there,
because cattle cannot be put on sage grass, because
it is not good
for them to eat, which means something to me about
belonging
and how my grandmother sits in her chair in a light
not so different
from the light that hits the curve on highway nine
with her hair
in rollers, and the TV going all day, and pasta drying
under the ceiling
fan, and her gnarled fingers softening and curling into
one another,
against which that same light lands as she dials
a number,
my number, which she has memorized, to hear my voice
say hello,
and to tell me that the pope is dying, and to ask me how
my girlfriend
is doing after the passing of her grandfather, which
is surprising,
and to say can you please order me more of that
body wash
they discontinued, because she does not have
the internet,
to which I say yes, of course, while I notice myself
drinking
her voice deep and thinking oh god, oh god, I love you,

I can't get far
enough away from it, and the time you held me
after I hit
my head so hard swinging under the big sweetgum
tree that
I pissed my pants carved such a hope in me that,
if I let it,
makes me feel strong and primally honest, which
is to say I too
have trumpets, and am toothless, and need somewhere
to land.

TRINKET X

today you are not
a rope of smoke
wrapped around
the moon no
you are not
a fleeting
opera of geese
slinging song
through the woods
from their secret
angles no
the work
you do is hard
but not unbearable
your life is swelling
over the estimation
you made of your life
you are not a piano
left to rot next to
the tabernacle not
the red poppy
in the wind not
the mute starlight
not the infinite place
behind your eyelids
not the bottle not
the knife not the saint
under the rose bush
not the salt white
broken wing
no you are not
allowed to assign
a length to your
tenderness but you
do need a voice
that loves you

ACKNOWLEDGMENTS & NOTES

The poems below or versions of the poems below have appeared or will appear in the following magazines:

"Unorganize This Mothership"/ *Waxwing*
"Hope Carves" / *Waxwing*
"Ozarks": / *poetry.onl*
"Trinket IX" / *like a field*
"You Say What's Wrong I Say an Eyelash" / Winner of 2023 Print Prize / *Columbia Journal*
"Florissant"/ *Gulf Coast*
"I Do Not Understand My Instrument" / *Missouri Review*

"Florissant" takes inspiration, in its discussion of the heart, from "Meditations in an Emergency" by Cameron Awkward-Rich.

The shape of "Unorganize This Mothership" is inspired by the poem "As Well as the Cicadas" by Guillaume Apollinaire.

"You Say What's Wrong I Say an Eyelash" takes its title from a line by Frank Stanford.

The image of the dogs' breath multiplying light in "I Do Not Understand My Instrument" takes inspiration from Richard Wright's 160th haiku in *Haiku: This Other World*.

The poems in *Trillion Amber Trumpets* would not exist without the love I've been lucky enough to share with my sister, my mother, my father, my nephew, my grandparents, my aunts, my uncles, and my cousins. You all wrote these poems with me my whole life, and I want you to know how much I love you.

Thank you to Kate, Bryan, and Seth for believing in my poems and for giving me a chance to put them out into the world in this way.

Thank you to Marguerite, janan, and Ty for their kind and moving words, always.

Thank you to Hope, Kwame, Stacey, Saddiq, Ross, Adrian, Cathy, Ty, Erin, Angie, Constance, Lydia, Maggie, David, Eszi, Ezra, Kassandra, Mannaseh, Luca, Abraham, Travis, Bernardo, Jess, Teja, Kourtney, and and and. You were the first readers for many of these poems, and I am forever in awe of your brilliance and generosity.

ABOUT THE POET

JC Andrews (she/her) is a lesbian poet from Springfield, Arkansas, with an interest in poems that hold questions as a form of caretaking. Her work can be found in *Gulf Coast*, *The Massachusetts Review*, *Salt Hill Journal*, and elsewhere. Her manuscript, *Of an Ilk*, was a finalist for the 2024 National Poetry Series, and her poem, "Gargoyle," was the first runner-up of the *Palette Poetry* 2024 Sappho Prize for Women Poets, judged by Megan Fernandes. She holds a B.A. in English-Creative Writing from Hendrix College in Conway, Arkansas, an MFA from Indiana University, and is currently a student and teacher at the University of Nebraska-Lincoln.

WWW.JCANDREWS.COM

ABOUT THE SERIES & PRESS

The Arkansas Queer Poet Series, proudly published by Sibling Rivalry Press, is dedicated to showcasing LGBTQ+ poets with a connection to Arkansas. Titles include:

Othered
by Randi M. Romo (AQPS #1)

Have You Seen This Man? The Castro Poems of Karl Tierney
edited by Jim Cory (AQPS #2)

Trillion Amber Trumpets
by JC Andrews (AQPS #3)

D I Y Body
by Toni Garcia-Butler (AQPS #4)

Listen, Kid: Selected & New Poems
by Bryan Borland (AQPS #5)

Sibling Rivalry Press is an independent press based in Little Rock, Arkansas, with a mission to publish work that disturbs and enraptures. It is a sponsored project of Fractured Atlas, a nonprofit arts service organization. Contributions to support the operations of Sibling Rivalry Press are tax-deductible to the extent permitted by law, and your donations will directly assist in the publication of work that disturbs and enraptures. To contribute to the publication of more books like this one, please visit our website and click *donate*.

WWW.SIBLINGRIVALRYPRESS.COM

www.ingramcontent.com/pod-product-compliance
Lightning Source LLC
LaVergne TN
LVHW041929090826
845145LV00017B/2770

* 9 7 8 1 9 4 3 9 7 7 9 3 2 *